# The Cremation
# of
# Sam McGee

## and other poems

## Robert W. Service

**Art Work by Mariken Van Nimwegen**

hancock

house

ISBN 0-88839-223-0
Copyright © 1989 Hancock House

**Canadian Cataloguing in Publication Data**

Service, Robert W., 1874 - 1958
  The Cremation of Sam McGee

ISBN 0-88839-223-0
I. Title.

PS8537.E78C74  1989    C811'.52    C89-091220-3
PR9199.3.S45C7  1989

Printed in Hong Kong

Published simultaneously in Canada and the United States by

HANCOCK HOUSE PUBLISHERS LTD.
19313 Zero Ave., Surrey, B.C.  V3S 5J9

HANCOCK HOUSE PUBLISHERS
1431 Harrison Ave., Blaine, WA 98230

# Table of Contents

# The Spell of the Yukon

I wanted the gold, and I sought it;
    I scrabbled and mucked like a slave.
Was it famine or scurvy, I fought it;
    I hurled my youth into a grave.
I wanted the gold, and I got it—
    Came out with a fortune last fall,—
Yet somehow life's not what I thought it,
    And somehow the gold isn't all.

No! There's the land. (Have you seen it?)
    It's the cussedest land that I know,
From the big, dizzy mountains that screen it
    To the deep, deathlike valleys below.
Some say God was tired when He made it;
    Some say it's a fine land to shun;
Maybe; but there's some as would trade it
    For no land on earth—and I'm one.

You come to get rich (damned good reason);
    You feel like an exile at first.
You hate it like hell for a season,
    And then you are worse than the worst.
It grips you like some kinds of sinning;

It twists you from foe to a friend;
It seems it's been since the beginning;
    It seems it will be to the end.

I've stood on some mighty-mouthed hollow
    That's plumb-full of hush to the brim.
I've watched the big, husky sun wallow
    In crimson and gold, and grow dim,
Till the moon set the pearly peaks gleaming,
    And the stars tumbled out, neck and crop;
And I've thought that I surely was dreaming,
    With the peace o' the world piled on top.

The summer—no sweeter was ever;
    The sunshiny woods all athrill;
The grayling aleap in the river,
    The bighorn asleep on the hill.
The strong life that never knows harness;
    The wilds where the caribou call;
The freshness, the freedom, the farness—
    O God, how I'm stuck on it all!

The winter! the brightness that blinds you,
    The white land locked tight as a drum,
The cold fear that follows and finds you,
    The silence that bludgeons you dumb.
The snows that are older than history,
    The woods where the weird shadows slant;
The stillness, the moonlight, the mystery,
    I've bade 'em good-bye—but I can't.

There's a land where the mountains are nameless,
    And the rivers all run God knows where;
There are lives that are erring and aimless,
    And deaths that just hang by a hair.
There are hardships that nobody reckons;
    There are valleys unpeopled and still;
There's a land—oh, it beckons and beckons,
    And I want to go back—and I will.

They're making my money diminish;
　　I'm sick of the taste of champagne.
Thank God! when I'm skinned to a finish
　　I'll pike to the Yukon again.
I'll fight—and you bet it's no sham-fight;
　　It's hell! but I've been there before;
And it's better than this by a damn sight—
　　So me for the Yukon once more.

There's gold, and it's haunting and haunting;
　　It's luring me on as of old;
Yet it isn't the gold that I'm wanting
　　So much as just finding the gold.
It's the great, big, broad land 'way up yonder,
　　It's the forests where silence has lease,
It's the beauty that thrills me with wonder,
　　It's the stillness that fills me with peace.

# My Friends

The man above was a murderer,
    the man below was a thief;
  And I lay there in the bunk between,
    ailing beyond belief;
A weary armful of skin and bone,
    wasted with pain and grief.

My feet were froze, and the lifeless toes
    were purple and green and gray.
  The little flesh that clung to my bones,
    you could punch in it holes like clay;
The skin on my gums was a sullen black,
    and slowly peeling away.

I was sure enough in a direful fix,
    and often I wondered why
  They did not take the chance that was left
    and leave me alone to die,
Or finish me off with a dose of dope—
    so utterly lost was I.

But no; they brewed me the green-spruce tea,
and nursed me there like a child;
And the homicide, he was good to me,
and bathed my sores and smiled;
And the thief, he starved that I might be fed,
and his eyes were kind and mild.

Yet they were woefully wicked men,
and often at night in pain
I heard the murderer speak of his deed
and dream it over again;
I heard the poor thief sorrowing for
the dead self he had slain.

I'll never forget that bitter dawn,
    so evil, askew and gray,
      When they wrapped me round in the skins of beasts
        and they bore me to a sleigh,
And we started out with the nearest post
    an hundred miles away.

I'll never forget the trail they broke,
    with its tense, unuttered woe;
      And the crunch, crunch, crunch as their snowshoes sank
        through the crust of the hollow snow;
And my breath would fail, and every beat
    of my heart was like a blow.

And oftentimes I would die the death,
    yet wake up to life anew;
      The sun would be all ablaze on the waste,
        and the sky a blighting blue,
And the tears would rise in my snow-blind eyes
    and furrow my cheeks like dew.

And the camps we made when their strength outplayed
    and the day was pinched and wan;
      And oh, the joy of that blessed halt,
        and how I did dread the dawn;
And how I hated the weary men
    who rose and dragged me on.

And oh, how I begged to rest, to rest—
    the snow was so sweet a shroud!
  And oh, how I cried when they urged me on,
    cried and cursed them aloud!
Yet on they strained, all racked and pained,
    and sorely their backs were bowed.

And then it was all like a lurid dream,
    and I prayed for a swift release
  From the ruthless ones who would not leave
    me to die alone in peace;
Till I wakened up and I found myself
    at the post of the Mounted Police.

And there was my friend the murderer,
    and there was my friend the thief,
  With bracelets of steel around their wrists,
    and wicked beyond belief:
But when they come to God's judgment seat—
    may I be allowed the brief.

# The Cremation of Sam McGee

*There are strange things done in the midnight sun*
*By the men who moil for gold;*
*The Arctic trails have their secret tales*
*That would make your blood run cold;*
*The Northern Lights have seen queer sights,*
*But the queerest they ever did see*
*Was that night on the marge of Lake Lebarge*
*I cremated Sam McGee.*

Now Sam McGee was from Tennessee,
where the cotton blooms and blows.
Why he left his home in the South to roam
'round the Pole, God only knows.
He was always cold, but the land of gold
seemed to hold him like a spell;
Though he'd often say in his homely way
that he'd "sooner live in Hell."

On a Christmas Day we were mushing our way
over the Dawson trail.
Talk of your cold! through the parka's fold
it stabbed like a driven nail.
If our eyes we'd close, then the lashes froze

till sometimes we couldn't see,
It wasn't much fun, but the only one
to whimper was Sam McGee.

And that very night, as we lay packed tight
in our robes beneath the snow,
And the dogs were fed, and the stars o'erhead
were dancing heel and toe,
He turned to me, and "Cap," says he,
"I'll cash in this trip, I guess;
And if I do, I'm asking that you
won't refuse my last request."

Well, he seemed so low that I couldn't say no;
then he says with a sort of moan,
"It's the cursed cold, and it's got right hold
till I'm chilled clean through to the bone.
Yet 'taint being dead—it's my awful dread
of the icy grave that pains;
So I want you to swear that, foul or fair,
you'll cremate my last remains."

A pal's last need is a thing to heed,
so I swore I would not fail;
And we started on at the streak of dawn;
but God! he looked ghastly pale.
He crouched on the sleigh, and he raved all day
of his home in Tennessee;
And before nightfall a corpse was all
that was left of Sam McGee.

There wasn't a breath in that land of death,
        and I hurried, horror-driven,
    With a corpse half hid that I couldn't get rid,
        because of a promise given;
It was lashed to the sleigh, and it seemed to say:
        "You may tax your brawn and brains,
    But you promised true, and it's up to you
        to cremate these last remains."


Now a promise made is a debt unpaid,
        and the trail has its own stern code.
    In the days to come, though my lips were dumb,
        in my heart how I cursed that load!
In the long, long night, by the lone firelight,
        while the huskies, round in a ring,
    Howled out their woes to the homeless snows—
        Oh God, how I loathed the thing!


And every day that quiet clay
        seemed to heavy and heavier grow;
    And on I went, though the dogs were spent
        and the grub was getting low.
The trail was bad, and I felt half mad,
        but I swore I would not give in;
    And I'd often sing to the hateful thing,
        and it hearkened with a grin.


Till I came to the marge of Lake Lebarge,
        and a derelict there lay;
    It was jammed in the ice, but I saw in a trice
        it was called the *Alice May.*
And I looked at it, and I thought a bit,

and I looked at my frozen chum;
Then "Here," said I, with a sudden cry,
    "is my cre-ma-tor-eum!"

Some planks I tore from the cabin floor,
        and I lit the boiler fire;
Some coal I found that was lying around,
        and I heaped the fuel higher;
The flames just soared, and the furnace roared—
        such a blaze you seldom see,
    And I burrowed a hole in the glowing coal,
        and I stuffed in Sam McGee.

Then I made a hike, for I didn't like
        to hear him sizzle so;
And the heavens scowled, and the huskies howled,
        and the wind began to blow.
It was icy cold, but the hot sweat rolled
        down my cheeks, and I don't know why;
    And the greasy smoke in an inky cloak
        went streaking down the sky.

I do not know how long in the snow
        I wrestled with grisly fear;
But the stars came out and they danced about
        ere again I ventured near;
I was sick with dread, but I bravely said,
        "I'll just take a peep inside.
    I guess he's cooked, and it's time I looked."
        Then the door I opened wide.

And there sat Sam, looking cool and calm,
    in the heart of the furnace roar;
And he wore a smile you could see a mile,
    and he said, "Please close that door.
It's fine in here, but I greatly fear
    you'll let in the cold and storm—
Since I left Plumtree, down in Tennessee,
    it's the first time I've been warm."

*There are strange things done in the midnight sun*
    *By the men who moil for gold;*
*The Arctic trails have their secret tales*
    *That would make your blood run cold;*
*The Northern Lights have seen queer sights,*
    *But the queerest they ever did see*
*Was that night on the marge of Lake Lebarge*
    *I cremated Sam McGee.*

# The Telegraph Operator

I will not wash my face;
   I will not brush my hair;
I "pig" around the place—
   There's nobody to care.
Nothing but rock and tree;
   Nothing but wood and stone,
Oh, God, it's hell to be
   Alone, alone, alone!

Snow-peaks and deep-gashed draws
   Corral me in a ring.
I feel as if I was
   The only living thing
On all this blighted earth;
   And so I frowst and shrink,
And crouching by my hearth
   I hear the thoughts I think.

I think of all I miss—
   The boys I used to know;
The girls I used to kiss;
   The coin I used to blow;
The bars I used to haunt;

The racket and the row;
The beers I didn't want
   (I wish I had 'em now).

Day after day the same,
   Only a little worse;
No one to grouch or blame—
   Oh, for a loving curse!
Oh, in the night I fear,
   Haunted by nameless things,
Just for a voice to cheer,
   Just for a hand that clings!

Faintly as from a star
   Voices come o'er the line;
Voices of ghosts afar,
   Not in this world of mine;

Lives in whose loom I grope;
    Words in whose weft I hear
Eager the thrill of hope,
    Awful the chill of fear.

I'm thinking out aloud;
    I reckon that is bad;
(The snow is like a shroud)—
    Maybe I'm going mad.
Say! wouldn't that be tough?

This awful hush that hugs
And chokes one is enough
    To make a man go "bugs."

There's not a thing to do;
    I cannot sleep at night;
No wonder I'm so blue;
    Oh, for a friendly fight!
The din and rush of strife;
    A music-hall aglow;
A crowd, a city, life—
    Dear God, I miss it so!

Here, you have moped enough!
    Brace up and play the game!
But say, it's awful tough—
    Day after day the same
(I've said that twice, I bet).
    Well, there's not much to say.
I wish I had a pet,
    Or something I could play.

Cheer up! don't get so glum
    And sick of everything.
The worst is yet to come;
    God help you till the Spring.
God shield you from the Fear;
    Teach you to laugh, not moan.
Ha! ha! it sounds so queer—
    Alone, alone, alone!

# Clancy of the Mounted Police

In the little Crimson Manual
    it's written plain and clear
    That who would wear the scarlet coat
      shall say good-bye to fear;
Shall be a guardian of the right,
    a sleuth-hound of the trail—
In the little Crimson Manual
    there's no such word as "fail"—
Shall follow on, though heavens fall,
    or Hell's top-turrets freeze,
Half round the world, if need there be,
    on bleeding hands and knees.

It's duty, duty, first and last,
    the Crimson Manual saith;
The Scarlet Riders make reply:
    "It's duty—to the death."
And so they sweep the solitudes,
    free men from all the earth;
And so they sentinel the woods,
    the wilds that know their worth;

And so they scour the startled plains
　　and mock at hurt and pain,
And read their Crimson Manual,
　　and find their duty plain.

Knights of the lists of unrenown,
　　born of the frontier's need,
Disdainful of the spoken word,
　　exultant in the deed;
Unconscious heroes of the waste,
　　proud players of the game,
Props of the power behind the throne,
　　upholders of the name;

For thus the Great White Chief hath said:
    "In all my lands be peace,"
And to maintain his word he gave
    his West the Scarlet Police.

Livid-lipped was the valley,
    still as the grave of God;
Misty shadows of mountain
    thinned into mists of cloud;
Corpselike and stark was the land,
    with a quiet that crushed and awed,
And the stars of the weird sub-arctic
    glimmered over its shroud.

Deep in the trench of the valley
    two men stationed the Post,
Seymour and Clancy the reckless,
    fresh from the long patrol;
Seymour, the sergeant, and Clancy—
    Clancy who made his boast
He could cinch like a bronco the Northland,
    and cling to the prongs of the Pole.

Two lone men on detachment,
    standing for law on the trail;
Undismayed in the vastness,
    wise with the wisdom of old—
Out of the night hailed a half-breed
    telling a pitiful tale:
"White man starving and crazy
    on the banks of the Nordenscold."

Up sprang the red-haired Clancy,
    lean and eager of eye;
Loaded the long toboggan,
    strapped each dog at its post;
Whirled his lash at the leader;
    then, with a whoop and a cry,
Into the Great White Silence
    faded away like a ghost.

The clouds were a misty shadow,
    the hills were a shadowy mist;
Sunless, voiceless and pulseless,
    the day was a dream of woe;
Through the ice-rifts the river
    smoked and bubbled and hissed;
Behind was a trail fresh broken,
    in front the untrodden snow.

Ahead of the dogs ploughed Clancy,
    haloed by steaming breath;
Through peril of open water,
    through ache of insensate cold;
Up rivers wantonly winding
    in a land affianced to death,
Till he came to a cowering cabin
    on the banks of the Nordenscold.

Then Clancy loosed his revolver,
    and he strode through the open door;
And there was the man he sought for,
    crouching beside the fire;

The hair of his beard was singeing,
    the frost on his back was hoar,
And ever he crooned and chanted
    as if he never would tire:—

*"I panned and I panned in the shiny sand,*
    *and I sniped on the river bar;*
*But I know, I know, that it's down below*
    *that the golden treasures are;*
*So I'll wait and wait till the floods abate,*
    *and I'll sink a shaft once more,*
*And I'd like to bet that I'll go home yet*
    *with a brass-band playing before."*

He was nigh as thin as a sliver,
    and he whined like a Moose-hide cur;
So Clancy clothed him and nursed him
    as a mother nurses a child;
Lifted him on the toboggan,
    wrapped him in robes of fur,
Then with the dogs sore straining
    started to face the Wild.

Said the Wild, "I will crush this Clancy,
    so fearless and insolent;
For him will I loose my fury,
    and blind and buffet and beat;
Pile up my snows to stay him;
    then when his strength is spent,
Leap on him from my ambush
    and crush him under my feet.

"Him will I ring with my silence,
    compass him with my cold;
Closer and closer clutch him
    unto mine icy breast;
Buffet him with my blizzards,
    deep in my snows enfold,
Claiming his life as my tribute,
    giving my wolves the rest."

Clancy crawled through the vastness;
    o'er him the hate of the Wild;
Full on his face fell the blizzard;
    cheering his huskies he ran;
Fighting, fierce-hearted and tireless,
    snows that drifted and piled,
With ever and ever behind him
    singing the crazy man:

*"Sing hey, sing ho, for the ice and snow,*
    *And a heart that's ever merry;*
*Let us trim and square with a lover's care*
    *—For why should a man be sorry?—*
*A grave deep, deep with the moon a-peep,*
    *A grave in the frozen mold.*
*Sing hey, sing ho, for the winds that blow,*
*And a grave deep down in the ice and snow,*
    *A grave in the land of gold."*

Day after day of darkness,
    the whirl of the seething snows;
Day after day of blindness,
    the swoop of the stinging blast;

On through a blur of fury
    the swing of staggering blows;
  On through a world of turmoil,
    empty, inane and vast.

Night with its writhing storm-whirl,
    night despairingly black;
  Night with its hours of terror,
    numb and endlessly long;
Night with its weary waiting,
    fighting the shadows back,
  And ever the crouching madman
    singing his crazy song.

Cold with its creeping terror,
    cold with its sudden clinch;
  Cold so utter you wonder
    if 'twill ever again be warm;
Clancy grinned as he shuddered,
    "Surely it isn't a cinch
  Being wet-nurse to a looney
    in the teeth of an arctic storm."

The blizzard passed and the dawn broke,
    knife-edged and crystal clear;
  The sky was a blue-domed iceberg,
    sunshine outlawed away;
Ever by snowslide and ice-rip
    haunted and hovered the Fear;
  Ever the Wild malignant
    poised and panted to slay.

The lead-dog freezes in harness—
    cut him out of the team!
The lung of the wheel-dog's bleeding—
    shoot him and let him lie!
On and on with the others—
    lash them until they scream!
"Pull for your lives, you devils!
    On! To halt is to die."

There in the frozen vastness
    Clancy fought with his foes;
The ache of the stiffened fingers,
    the cut of the snowshoe thong;
Cheeks black-raw through the hood-flap,
    eyes that tingled and closed,
And ever to urge and cheer him
    quavered the madman's song.

Colder it grew and colder,
    till the last heat left the earth,
And there in the great stark stillness
    the bale fires glinted and gleamed,
And the Wild all around exulted
    and shook with a devilish mirth,
And life was far and forgotten,
    the ghost of a joy once dreamed.

Death! And one who defied it,
    a man of the Mounted Police;
Fought it there to a standstill
    long after hope was gone;
Grinned through his bitter anguish,
    fought without let or cease,
Suffering, straining, striving,
    stumbling, struggling on,

Till the dogs lay down in their traces,
    and rose and staggered and fell;
Till the eyes of him dimmed with shadows,
    and the trail was so hard to see;
Till the Wild howled out triumphant,
    and the world was a frozen hell—
Then said Constable Clancy:
    "I guess that it's up to me."

Far down the trail they saw him,
 and his hands, they were blanched like bone;
His face was a blackened horror,
 from his eye-lids the salt rheum ran.
His feet he was lifting strangely,
 as if they were made of stone,
But safe in his arms and sleeping
 he carried the crazy man.

So Clancy got into Barracks,
 and the boys made rather a scene;
And the O.C. called him a hero,
 and was nice as a man could be;
But Clancy gazed down his trousers
 at the place where his toes had been,
And then he howled like a husky,
 and sang in a shaky key:

*"When I go back to the old love*
 *that's true to the finger-tips,*
*I'll say: 'Here's bushels of gold, love,'*
 *and I'll kiss my girl on the lips;*
*'It's yours to have and to hold, love.'*
 *It's the proud, proud boy I'll be,*
*When I go back to the old love*
 *that's waited so long for me."*

# The Ballad of Hard Luck Henry

Now wouldn't you expect to find
    a man an awful crank
That's staked out nigh three hundred claims,
    and every one a blank;
That's followed every fool stampede,
    and seen the rise and fall
Of camps where men got gold in chunks
    and he got none at all;
That's prospected a bit of ground
    and sold it for a song
To see it yield a fortune to
    some fool that came along;
That's sunk a dozen bedrock holes,
    and not a speck in sight,
Yet sees them take a million
    from the claims to left and right?
Now aren't things like that enough
    to drive a man to booze?
But Hard-Luck Smith was hoodoo-proof—
    he knew the way to lose.

'Twas in the fall of nineteen-four—
    leap-year, I've heard them say—
When Hard-Luck came to Hunker Creek
    and took a hillside lay.
And lo! as if to make amends
    for all the futile past,
Late in the year he struck it rich,
    the real pay-streak at last.
The riffles of his sluicing-box
    were choked with speckled earth,
And night and day he worked that lay
    for all that he was worth.
And when in chill December's gloom
    his lucky lease expired,
He found that he had made a stake
    as big as he desired.

One day while meditating on
    the waywardness of fate,
He felt the ache of lonely man
    to find a fitting mate;
A petticoated pard to cheer
    his solitary life,
A woman with soft, soothing ways,
    a confidante, a wife.
And while he cooked his supper
    on his little Yukon stove,
He wished that he had staked a claim
    in Love's rich treasure-trove;
When suddenly he paused and held
    aloft a Yukon egg,

For there in pencilled letters
   was the magic name of Peg.

You know these Yukon eggs of ours—
   some pink, some green, some blue—
A dollar per, assorted tints, assorted flavors, too!
The supercilious cheechako
   might designate them high,
But one acquires a taste for them
   and likes them by-and-by.
Well, Hard-Luck Henry took this egg
   and held it to the light,
And there was more faint pencilling
   that sorely taxed his sight.
At last he made it out, and then
   the legend ran like this—
"Will Klondike miner write to Peg,
   Plumhollow, Squashville, Wis.?"

That night he got to thinking of
   this far-off, unknown fair;
It seemed so sort of opportune,
   an answer to his prayer.
She flitted sweetly through his dreams,
   she haunted him by day,
She smiled through clouds of nicotine,
   she cheered his weary way.
At last he yielded to the spell;
   his course of love he set—
Wisconsin his objective point,
   his object, Margaret.

With every mile of sea and land
  his longing grew and grew.
 He practiced all his pretty words,
  and these, I fear, were few.
At last, one frosty evening,
  with a cold chill down his spine,
 He found himself before her house,
  the threshold of the shrine.
His courage flickered to a spark,
  then glowed with sudden flame.
 He knocked; he heard a welcome word;
  she came—his goddess came!
Oh, she was fair as any flower,
  and huskily he spoke:
  "I'm all the way from Klondike, with
  a mighty heavy poke.
I'm looking for a lassie, one
  whose Christian name is Peg,
 Who sought a Klondike miner,
  and who wrote it on an egg."

 The lassie gazed at him a space,
  her cheeks grew rosy red.
 She gazed at him with tear-bright eyes,
  then tenderly she said:
"Yes, lonely Klondike miner,
  it is true my name is Peg.
 It's also true I longed for you
  and wrote it on an egg.
My heart went out to someone in
  that land of night and cold;

But oh, I fear that Yukon egg
    must have been mighty old.
I waited long, I hoped and feared;
    you should have come before;
I've been a wedded woman now
    for eighteen months or more.
I'm sorry, since you've come so far,
    you ain't the one that wins;
But won't you take a step inside?—
    I'll let you see the twins!"

# Premonition

'Twas a year ago and the moon was bright
    (Oh, I remember so well, so well);
I walked with my love in a sea of light,
    And the voice of my sweet was a silver bell.
        And sudden the moon grew strangely dull,
           And sudden my love had taken wing;
        I looked on the face of a grinning skull,
           I strained to my heart a ghastly thing.

'Twas but fantasy, for my love lay still
    In my arms, with her tender eyes aglow,
And she wondered why my lips were chill,
    Why I was silent and kissed her so.
        A year has gone and the moon is bright,
           A gibbous moon, like a ghost of woe;
        I sit by a new-made grave tonight,
           And my heart is broken—it's strange, you know.

# The Ballad of Blasphemous Bill

I took a contract to bury the body
    of blasphemous Bill MacKie,
    Whenever, wherever or whatsoever
    the manner of death he die—
Whether he die in the light o' day
    or under the peak-faced moon;
    In cabin or dance-hall, camp or dive,
    mucklucks or patent shoon;
On velvet tundra or virgin peak,
    by glacier, drift or draw;
    In muskeg hollow or canyon gloom,
    by avalanche, fang or claw;
By battle, murder or sudden wealth,
    by pestilence, "hooch" or lead—
    I swore on the Book I would follow and look
    till I found my tombless dead.

For Bill was a dainty kind of cuss,
    and his mind was mighty sot
On a dinky patch with flowers and grass
    in a civilized boneyard lot.
And where he died or how he died,
    it didn't matter a damn

So long as he had a grave with frills
    and a tombstone epigram.
So I promised him, and he paid the price
    in good cheechako coin
    (Which the same I blowed on that very night
    down in the Tenderloin).
Then I painted a three-foot slab of pine:
    "Here lies poor Bill MacKie,"
And I hung it up on my cabin wall
    and I waited for Bill to die.

Years passed away, and at last one day
    came a squaw with a story strange,
Of a long-deserted line of traps
    'way back of the Bighorn range;
Of a little hut by the great divide,
    and a white man stiff and still,
Lying there by his lonesome self,
    and I figured it must be Bill.
So I thought of the contract I'd made with him,
    and I took down from the shelf
The swell black box with the silver plate
    he'd picked out for hisself;
And I packed it full of grub and "hooch,"
    and I slung it on the sleigh;
Then I harnessed up my team of dogs
    and was off at dawn of day.

You know what it's like in the Yukon wild
    when it's sixty-nine below;
When the ice-worms wriggle their purple heads
    through the crust of the pale blue snow;

When the pine trees crack like little guns
    in the silence of the wood,
  And the icicles hang down like tusks
    under the parka hood;
When the stovepipe smoke breaks sudden off,
    and the sky is weirdly lit,
  And the careless feel of a bit of steel
    burns like a red-hot spit;
When the mercury is a frozen ball,
    and the frost-fiend stalks to kill—
  Well, it was just like that that day
    when I set out to look for Bill.

Oh, the awful hush that seemed to crush
    me down on every hand,
  As I blundered blind with a trail to find
    through that blank and bitter land;
Half dazed, half crazed in the winter wild,
    with its grim heart-breaking woes,
  And the ruthless strife for a grip on life
    that only the sourdough knows!
North by the compass, North I pressed;
    river and peak and plain
  Passed like a dream I slept to lose
    and I waked to dream again.

River and plain and mighty peak—
    and who could stand unawed?
  As their summits blazed, he could stand undazed
    at the foot of the throne of God.
North, aye, North, through a land accurst,
    shunned by the scouring brutes,

And all I heard was my own harsh word
        and the whine of the malamutes,
Till at last I came to a cabin squat,
        built in the side of a hill,
    And I burst in the door, and there on the floor,
        frozen to death, lay Bill.

Ice, white ice, like a winding-sheet,
        sheathing each smoke-grimed wall;
    Ice on the stove-pipe, ice on the bed,
        ice gleaming over all;
Sparkling ice on the dead man's chest,
        glittering ice in his hair,
    Ice on his fingers, ice in his heart,
        ice in his glassy stare;

Hard as a log and trussed like a frog,
    with his arms and legs outspread.
I gazed at the coffin I'd brought for him,
    and I gazed at the gruesome dead,
And at last I spoke; "Bill liked his joke;
    but still, goldarn his eyes,
A man had ought to consider his mates
    in the way he goes and dies."

Have you ever stood in an Arctic hut
    in the shadow of the pole,
With a little coffin six by three
    and a grief you can't control?
Have you ever sat by a frozen corpse
    that looks at you with a grin,
And that seems to say: "You may try all day,
    but you'll never jam me in?"
I'm not a man of the quitting kind,
    but I never felt so blue
As I sat there gazing at that stiff
    and studying what I'd do.
Then I rose and I kicked off the husky dogs
    that were nosing round about,
And I lit a roaring fire in the stove,
    and I started to thaw Bill out.

Well, I thawed and thawed for thirteen days,
    but it didn't seem no good;
His arms and legs stuck out like pegs,
    as if they was made of wood.
Till at last I said: "It ain't no use—
    he's froze too hard to thaw;

He's obstinate, and he won't lie straight,
    so I guess I got to—saw."
So I sawed off poor Bill's arms and legs,
    and I laid him snug and straight
In the little coffin he picked hisself,
    with the dinky silver plate;
And I came nigh to near shedding a tear
    as I nailed him safely down;
    Then I stowed him away in my Yukon sleigh,
    and I started back to town.

So I buried him as the contract called
    in a narrow grave and deep,
And there he's waiting the Great Clean-up,
    when the Judgment sluice-heads sweep;
And I smoke my pipe and I meditate
    in the light of the Midnight Sun,
And sometimes I wonder if they *was,*
    the awful things I done.
And as I sit and the parson talks,
    expounding on the Law,
I often think of poor old Bill—
    and how hard he was to saw.

# The Heart of the Sourdough

There, where the mighty mountains bare
      their fangs unto the moon,
There, where the sullen sun-dogs glare
      in the snow-bright, bitter noon,
And the glacier-gutted streams sweep down
      at the clarion call of June.

There, where the livid tundras keep
      their tryst with the tranquil snows;
There, where the silences are spawned,
      and the light of hell-fire flows
Into the bowl of the midnight sky, violet, amber and rose.

There, where the rapids churn and roar,
      and the ice-floes bellowing run;
Where the tortured, twisted rivers of blood
      rush to the setting sun—
I've packed my kit and I'm going, boys,
      ere another day is done.

I knew it would call, or soon or late,
      as it calls the whirring wings;
It's the olden lure, it's the golden lure,

it's the lure of the timeless things,
And tonight, oh, God of the trails untrod,
how it whines in my heart-strings!

I'm sick to death of your well-groomed gods,
your make-believe and your show;
I long for a whiff of bacon and beans,
a snug shakedown in the snow;
A trail to break, and a life at stake,
and another bout with the foe.

With the raw-ribbed Wild that abhors all life,
the Wild that would crush and rend,
I have clinched and closed with the naked North,
I have learned to defy and defend;
Shoulder to shoulder we have fought it out—
yet the Wild must win in the end.

I have flouted the Wild. I have followed its lure,
fearless, familiar, alone;
By all that the battle means and makes
I claim that land for mine own;
Yet the Wild must win, and a day will come
when I shall be overthrown.

Then when, as wolf-dogs fight, we've fought,
the lean wolf-land and I;
Fought and bled till the snows are red
under the reeling sky;
Even as lean wolf-dogs go down
will I go down and die.

# The Three Voices

The waves have a story to tell me,
    As I lie on the lonely beach;
Chanting aloft in the pine-tops,
    The wind has a lesson to teach;
But the stars sing an anthem of glory
    I cannot put into speech.

The waves tell of ocean spaces,
    Of hearts that are wild and brave,
Of populous city places,
    Of desolate shores they lave,
Of men who sally in quest of gold
    To sink in an ocean grave.

The wind is a mighty roamer;
    He bids me keep me free,
Clean from the taint of the gold-lust,
    Hardy and pure as he;
Cling with my love to nature
    As a child to the mother knee.

But the stars throng out in their glory,
    And they sing of the God in man;
They sing of the Mighty Master,
    Of the loom His fingers span,
Where a star or a soul is a part of the whole,
    And weft in the wondrous plan.

Here by the camp-fire's flicker,
    Deep in my blanket curled,
I long for the peace of the pine-gloom,
    When the scroll of the Lord is unfurled,
And the wind and the wave are silent,
    And world is singing to world.